Truc Tran: My Story of a District Attorney in War

The Vietnam War (1975) put an end to the shooting, but the terrors and tortures in what were dubbed "Re-education Camps" for the surrendered were hell on earth every day for many years. The "Hanoi Hilton" for American POWs is evidence of such terrors and tortures.

Truc Tran & Winston Vo

Copyright © 2023

All Rights Reserved

Dedication

As living through the war(s), you would hope for peace, and even accept the odds. My uncle Truc now talks with highly sarcasm, while my dad So is live on. When you read stories like this, you feel the devastation and suffering of jumping into an unjustified hell on earth for not a day, but for years like that.

It is a chess war exchanged between two Political Blocs- the Communism was leaded by China and Soviet, while the Capitalism was leaded by The United States. The US lost a lot of man in the Vietnam War in a 20-year armed conflicts, not easy to walk away.

The chess table was then falling over South Korea and West Germany.

Without any reservation, each country that once participated in fighting along with the United States, now gives a traditional ceremony each year for The South Vietnam Armed Forces with full decorated uniforms, not be seen at other nations communities. The lost and struggles in the Communists Re-education Camps and the risks of fleeing on the Ocean are now overdue.

Winston Vo

Acknowledgment

My uncle Truc wrote a manuscript of this book- fully edited in 2003. I have thought of authoring a book to recount my times with these two speculator lawyers- my uncle Truc and my dad So. They were left behind the country and spent many terrible years in the Re-education Camps by the Communists. I had raised my attention about the influential works that these two persons made but did not persuade me its high stake or anyone if I had a chance to meet. My uncle has a high profile and people are in debt to him, but my dad So is completely out of sight- a hand in the education system, and a hand in the Army- All are superficial at its power. Yeah! in -- /1975, he was approved for joining The Office of The Military Attache- (Major General) in Saigon but waived for my youngest sister soon to be born- April 7, 1975, in Vung Tau. That is a high post and influential, but not in place yet!

I had a great editing team managed by Jenna West. My uncle is a highly amused person, especially with an English/French language, and your input is needed to assure me that: "It's all-American authentic sayings."

Winston Vo

Contents

Dedication iii

Acknowledgment iv

Prologue vii

My Name 1

My Homeland 2

My Family 3

My Disappointment 7

My Culture 8

My Wars 9

My View of United States Involvement in the Vietnam War 13

My View of Communism 21

My Elusive Nightmare 27

My Wife 31

My Education 32

My Incarceration 38

My First Attempt at Re-Location 44

My Nine Years as a Prisoner of War 53

My Release from Prison 61

My Mercantile Adventure 65

My Nashville Home 68

About The Author 74

Prologue

Winston Hieu-Duc Vo, a chemical engineer schooled at Vanderbilt and Johns Hopkins. The author- Mr. Truc Tran is my uncle.

The flock of demonstrators rushed into the gate and the wall of Berlin. The guards were waiting for orders from their commanders. Look at the Tiananmen Square in China; the tanks ran over the demonstrators. It was so inhuman, but the world and, especially, the American government was not alarmed about it. If we made it a big deal, especially bringing it into the international court will make a mindset for an action, not hesitation as right now. President Bush, Sr was the President at that time. He once was the Ambassador to China, and even before that, he was the Director of the CIA. That was a fortune for all things in place, and Germany was unified. The fall of Eastern Europe Communism was a domino's effect.

The other part of Asia, South Korea made, a spectacular Olympic 1988 in Seoul. We were sad for South Vietnam once prospective.

The Vietnam War after 1975 actually still was going on in different dimensions. American troops withdrew in 1973, and the advisory was still on the ground until 1975. It was not a civil war of a country, but for two blocks of political doctrines- where they exchanged on the battlefield here in Vietnam. We are still confused as to why we let South Korean troops fighting here in South Vietnam, which made our people think of it as "a bad foreign intervention", and Vietnam just were liberated from the French, with bad memoirs.

A 2-year period after the American Troop's withdrawal was enough time to make a post-war plan. The built-up strong South Vietnam's army now was hard to deter. The overthrow of the government or change of leadership were happening anytime. We had prepared for an option to retreat to the deep south with Phu Quoc Island, a model of Taiwan to offense but not a leader or general to execute it yet. A newly installed president- Major General Duong Van Minh, who once ordered to kill of President Ngo Dinh Diem, aligned with President Kennedy's agreement, looked like we had to stay and fight; instead, he ordered the army to surrender the Communists unconditionally in a few days into office.

The withdrawal from the Central Highland (Pleiku and Kon-Tum) was a test for American troops to intervene, which turned into a disaster.

The ace was played at high profiles: Truc Tran and his brother-in-law So Huu Vo, in a game which both knew nothing about. Both were lawyers, but their youth and roots were camouflaged with the working class (farmers) of their parents in the village.

In 1981, participants on both sides of the Vietnam War began a retrospective on how the War and South Vietnam Government went down so quickly.

The following year, in 1982, my dad- So Huu Vo, was released (7 years) from "Re-education Camp" (prison is a better term). My uncle- Truc Tran, was released 2 years later in 1984 (9 years). My uncle Truc bought a house in Saigon on arrival (1975) from the running out of the Central Region- Hue. Now, he let my dad live in this house with him, which was designed for 3 families with different entrances. My mom and kids were still staying in Hue. I came to visit him one summer, then stayed over, planning to get out of the country by boat. My uncle Truc kept changing his plan, so he never made it here. It turned out good that my dad had me by his side, and astonishment that my life was changed totally upside down from a poor academic performance to being on top of my class in only one summer.

My dad- So Huu Vo, now was transformed and succeeded in this new society: an electronic instructor at The Electronics Apprenticeship School at Dakao (District 1, Saigon) (Truong Dien Tu Dakao), where my dad's student-owned it, and gave him books to learn and furthermore, my dad was a well merchant. To get support for a residency in Saigon, he registered with an elite academic group, named Center for Research and Translation Services (Trung Tam Nghien Cuu va Dich Thuat) with many other activities in a very decent compound in District 3, Saigon. He started with a social studies group, in which he was excellent for his reports on Culture, Drug Traffic, and Prostitution, which were considered as a product of Capitalism. After this assignment, he continued to keep a membership while doing other private businesses. At once, they opened a session of "A Refreshment Course about Socialism for High-Ranking Cadres." At this time, my dad's residency status (in Saigon) was still illegal, so my dad wanted to enroll in. There were a lot of field trips, critiques of the movies, and a thesis at the end. My dad's thesis was about "Analyze "The Tale of Kieu by Nguyen Du" under The Scope of Marxist-Leninist" (Phan Tich "Truyen Kieu" Duoi Cai Nhin Cua Chu Nghia Marxist-Leninist). At the end of this course, he was ranked 1st and honored to deliver a speech at its commencement address. Things that would cause a "crisis" (at global) if it were televised and printed on the newspaper with a subject like "a high-ranking member of South Vietnam Government was inspired (Cam Hoa) by Marxist-Leninist. The Head of Instructors was President HoChiMinh's Personal Adviser, not present at that ceremony either. That was in 1987. It would be a boost for Socialism around the World, and South Korea's Olympics (in 1988) would be affected.

Another event not less important: Medical Doctor Tran Dong A (was once in re-education camp after 1975) succeeded in operating a pair of two boys: Viet-Duc, which was phenomenal by that time. Here, the name of the two boys was shown as a collaboration of Viet - Duc (Vietnam - East Germany).

Another, a former South Vietnam officer, with the rank of Captain, was featured by this time in Saigon for his success in exporting a garment- a model of the private sector.

Those three events (stories) would not only bring in a new era of collateral for the South Vietnamese's Regime, but also further boosted the success of Socialism after the dark (failure) of the economy and boat peoples (refugees) over Southeast Asia.

That at least could firmly open fire into the East Germany's demonstrators rush into the gates at the Berlin Wall.

I at first was critiquing my uncle Truc, but it was hard to start or cover things in a memoir, and things were not clearly meant as described, especially no sides (countries) leaving a trace. Our folk says we are, unfortunately, the buyers from gangs selling "Wild (flying) Duck. Wait until dark to take them home!" That is reserved for a dialog and interview with different parts of our life, and interviews with my uncle's friends.

Winston Hieu-Duc Vo

Nashville, Tennessee (USA)

September 15, 2023

Notes: Things to think about Vietnam:

India's Gandhi: a leader of India's nonviolent independence movement against British rule (in 1947).

French Colonists: (in 1945) the French mainland was occupied by German, but still returned to colonize Indochina (Vietnam-Laos-Cambodia) until 1954 after losing at the Dien Bien Phu Battle.

China's Prime Minister Dang Tieu Binh was visiting the United States in 1979: "will teach Vietnam a lesson" for overthrowing Khmer Rouge!

****

Some sketched CV of my uncle- Truc Tran

A Candidate (1996) for Legal Counsel

for the US Embassy in Hanoi

Before 1975

Bachelor of Law (Cu Nhan Luat) in Hue University-School of Law, 1964

Prosecutor at Military Courts in Quang Tri & Hue Provinces

District Attorney (Bien Ly) in Quy Nhon and Hue Provinces

After released from the Re-education Camp in 1984 (9 years)

Legal Advisor for Joint Stock Electronics Tien-Dat Company

Staff Lawyer for Russin & Vecchi Law Firm

Instructor in Contract Law at Open University (a British model) in Saigon.

Permitted to immigrate to the United States in 1995 with his daughter (at first, for study purpose). His wife still stayed in Vietnam.

Arriving in the United States in 1995

A Candidate (1996) for Legal Counsel for the US Embassy in Hanoi with supports from Dr. Bahr Weiss, a Psychology Professor at Vanderbilt University; Mr. Bob Clement, a US Representative from Tennessee; and Vecchi- a partner of Russin & Vecchi Law Firm in Saigon.

****

Some sketched CV of my dad- So Huu Vo

Before 1975

(Born from a farmer's family in a village in Hue.)

Quoc Hoc, Hue (1957)

Bachelor of Law (Cu Nhan Luat) in Hue University- School of Law (1959-ranked 1st & 1968)

Principal of Bo-De (Buddhist) High School in Quang Tri Province (1959-1966) at the age of 24.

Elected as Head Representative (Khoa 22- Khoa Tong Dong Vien) Thu-Duc Military Academy (1966)

Chief- Judicial Military Police (MP) in Quang Tri - Hue - DaNang

Principal of Van Hoa Quan Doi in DaNang (school for Militants' children) (1971-1975); in -- /1975, approved for joining The Office of The Military Attache- (Major General) in Saigon but waived for my youngest sister soon to be born- April 7, 1975, in Vung Tau. Cindy Ngan-Ha Vo now, is a pharmacist in Montreal, Canada. (PharmD, Mercer University 2002)

After released from the Re-education Camp in 1982 (7 years)

A merchant for schooler and worker's backpacks

Joined in as a member (Social Studies) of an elite academic group, named Center for Research and Translation Services (Trung Tam Nghien Cuu va Dich Thuat), District 3, Saigon

Electronic Instructor at The Electronics Apprenticeship School at Dakao (District 1, Saigon)

(My dad's student was the owner, and gave him books for self-study)

Enrolled in "A Refreshment Course about Socialism for High-Ranking Cadres" at the above center (my dad's residency status (in Saigon) was still illegal) with a thesis: "Analyze The Tale of Kieu by Nguyen Du" under The Scope of Marxist-Leninist"

Dad was ranked 1st and was honored to deliver a speech at its commencement address.

Joined in a new business of Newspapers and Books Wholesaler, and leased a Book Boutique next to Gia Long High School

Refused to be a partner with a graduate from School of Business Administration (Quoc Gia Hanh Chanh) to open a legal service. My dad has a law degree but has not practiced yet under the South Vietnam Government.

Immigrated to the United States in 1992 under The H.O. (#13) Program.

TRUC TRAN: My Story of a District Attorney in War

My Name

My name is Truc Tran and this is my story. I was born in Hue, Vietnam, on September 19, 1938. My parents put their ambition in my name. They wanted me to be a good man and do good things.

Truc means bamboo. The Bamboo plant, in Asia, is the symbol of a gentleman. Bamboo is a long, tall tree that is composed of segments of cylinders. If you split a segment, there is nothing in it.

In Vietnam, Bamboo represents a gentleman because a gentleman does what he is meant to do. He finds a void and fills it. A gentleman does things just because he needs to. Not because of the materialistic benefit he gets from doing it. But for what, his soul benefits from completing the task. I try to fulfill my parents' wish. I am a good man.

I am happy to tell my story. I appreciate your interest in reading it. I need to tell it. The world needs to know what really happened. I will talk to you about what I think is the policy of the United States Armed Forces. I think they are very talented. They have a great brain. I have heard some people over here say that it was a mistake to be involved in the Vietnam War.

I said, "No! Everything that was done was good for the United States. I will tell you about it."

Truc Tran & Winston Vo

My Homeland

Many of you know of my homeland. But you do not know the nature of the land I lived and loved. My country homeland is nestled in a tropical, temperate zone characterized by strong monsoon influences. A considerable amount of sun, a high rainfall rate, and high humidity cause this region to be endowed with a temperate climate.

Our hot season occurs from May to October. We do have a cold season, which arises from November to April. However, the difference in temperature between the two seasons in southern Vietnam is almost unnoticeable, averaging 3 degrees C.

My city of birth, Hue, is located centrally along the coast of my homeland. Hue is the ancient capital of the last dynasty.

My Family

My father's name is Oanh Tran. He was born in a poor village south of Hue. He was a rice farmer. When he was born, 90% of Vietnamese providers were farmers. We ate a lot of rice.

My father's family was very poor. When his father died, he had to leave the village to help support his family. He moved to town. In town, he ran a laundry. Most of his employees were our relatives or people from our village. He farmed and ran the laundry. This is where he met my mother.

Eventually, this business brought him a lot of money. I can remember that year. It was a happy year. We had plenty of expensive clothes. I ate chocolate. Chocolate was very expensive in Vietnam at that time. Yes, I remember that year. But I also remember the winter was very, very bad. It rained for three months. It always rains too much. It was very cold every morning when I woke up.

I remember one particular morning when my grandmother carried me to a big fire in the middle of the house. I remember her searching for new clothes for me because I wet myself during the night. These memories are of a peaceful and happy life. I remember a peaceful and happy life... until 1945.

My father sent me to French Catholic schools. The first Catholic school I attended, Ecole Pellerin, was established by the

Brothers of Jean Baptist de la Salle. It was a very nice school. A lot of high-ranking officials of the government attended that school. The school was academically strong. My siblings were less fortunate. They attended public school.

My parents spent a lot of money for me to attend a French Catholic school. It was very expensive to go to that school, so the rest of my siblings had to go to public school. My youngest brother, the one who died in the general attack in 1968, went to the French Catholic School. My two middle siblings went to public school.

I began to learn French. I tried to learn some Latin, but it was challenging. I chose to study Vietnamese and French. I also learned English in this school. I remember that year. I have a good memory. This was a time when the French had control of Vietnam.

Later, my mother's small business paid for me and my sibling to attend a private Catholic School named Institut de la Providence. It would have taken more than half of my father's salary to send us. I was fortunate to be able to go to a Catholic school. My parents did not have much of an education.

We came to the city in 1949. My father worked for a railroad company. My mother had a café. She sold drinks and food to French soldiers. She earned enough money to continue to send me to the Catholic school. The tuition was very high to attend there.

I have one brother and two sisters. I am the oldest of my

parents' four children. This is not a big family for Vietnamese. The typical size of a Vietnamese family is four or five children.

In 1944, my sister, Ngan Tran, was born. My parent's third child, Hong Tran, was born in 1947. My brother, Giau Tran, is the youngest. He was born in 1949. My parents took care in naming their children. All Vietnamese names have meaning.

Ngan means gold. My father named my sister Ngan because gold is very precious. He wanted her to be a good wife who does everything for her husband and her children. He wanted her to do her best to benefit society as well. My sister, Ngan, graduated from high school, then went on attending a teacher's school. She was a middle school teacher. Her husband was a lawyer. She presently works in a Walmart store in Nashville, Tennessee.

Hong means rose, pretty, beautiful. Hong got some education and got married. She is a housewife. She remains in Vietnam with her family.

Giau means rich. When Giau was born, my parents were very poor. They put their wish to have enough money in his name.

My wife was born in 1945. Her name is Nga. Nga means beautiful girl. My wife was beautiful when she was young. She still lives in Vietnam.

When I came to the United States in 1995, she was on the

refugee list to come with me. But she was too weak to fly such a long way at that time. She also was reluctant to leave her sick mother in Vietnam. The Vietnamese have a custom. The Vietnamese maintains a tradition of caring for aging parents. When the parents die, we pray for their souls to enter heaven.

In 2003, I submitted an application for her to come to the United States. I thought she would come, but she changed her mind. She changes her mind often. She wrote to me to say she would not come. She was too scared. Coming to the United States is very scary for someone in their sixties. The change in culture would be hard to adjust to.

My wife and I have one daughter. She was born in 1974. Her name is Tran Tran. Tran means precious. She received her master's degree in economics at Middle Tennessee State University. She recently married. And now, my life begins to live for myself.

I have one sister who lives over here. She came here because her husband was a lawyer and Captain in the South Vietnamese Army. After we lost the War in 1975, they put her husband in prison for seven years. Me, for nine years. Because of our involvement in the Vietnam War against the Communists.

My Disappointment

My mother died of tuberculosis in 1962. Tuberculosis was curable at that time, but my family was very poor and could not afford medical treatment.

I was 22 years old when my mother died. I was in my second year of Law School.

I knew she was going to die. This is when the Vietnam War was very terrible. The War was beginning to escalate. The nation had to mobilize all its human resources for the War. I was given a job as a clerk in the court. I showed my mother the papers that called me to take the court clerk position while she was in the hospital. She cried. She cried because she thought I had lied to her. She thought I was going to War and that I lied about the court clerk position. She didn't want me to join the army. She died one week before I took the job. It broke my heart. This was very difficult for me. I was unable to please my mother. But my mother knows now, in the afterlife, what really happened.

My Culture

The Vietnamese were very, very poor people. There was a lot of famine due to the bad weather. People were starving. Their diet depended on what was available for eating. Along with rice, we ate fish and vegetables. Occasionally, we ate red meat. Mostly, we ate chicken, beef, and pork.

In the poorest villages in the northern part of Vietnam, the weather was very bad. There was a lot of famine. So, if there were no crops to eat, people ate anything they could find to eat. Even cats and dogs. Only because they were very hungry.

Some Vietnamese believe in an afterlife. They believe that when they die, a dog leads them to the best place in the afterlife. These Vietnamese do not eat dogs. They love dogs. Catholics did not believe this story. Sometimes, they ate cats or dogs.

The majority of Vietnamese people do not eat dogs and cats and they do not respect those who do. Most who eat dogs today are people who overindulge in their eating habits.

TRUC TRAN: My Story of a District Attorney in War

My Wars

I was born in 1938, one year before World War II began. I want you to understand that over half of my life experience has been during a war. More than half of my life. After one War, there was always another war. What we suffered from the War I remember very well. Before I was aware of my surroundings, when my father had his laundry, my life was wonderful.

I remember the year I started learning English. That year, in the mornings when I would be going to school, I would see Japanese soldiers pass in front of my house. My uncles and their friends tried to steal weapons from them. When the soldiers would get in their car to go somewhere, they would jump in the car and grab their guns. When my uncles talked about the resistance against France, I wasn't listening.

When I grew older and started studying history, I realized at that time, most of the Vietnamese people were fighting against the French to gain independence. I learned the stories I heard my uncles telling, were stories of my uncles trying to overcome the French occupation to gain independence from them. I loved my uncles because of that.

After the surrender of Japan to its allies in 1945, the French tried to reoccupy Vietnam. My uncles enlisted in the army to fight against the French. These were my mother's brothers. My father only had one younger brother. He fought as a soldier in the South Vietnamese Army against the Communists.

When the French had reoccupied my home city in 1945, we had to evacuate my village. It was a very, very hard year because the Japanese ordered us not to grow rice. Farmers could not grow rice. We did not have enough rice to eat. We had almost nothing to eat. The Japanese established plants that were used for industry. Most of the Vietnamese people did not have anything to eat. I remember that.

I cannot remember everything that happened in 1947. I was too young. But what I do remember is when the French came, we had to go from the farm to the village. I remember one night, we had nothing to eat. My father disappeared into the night and returned with two cans of rice. He boiled the rice in a pan with a lot of water. He made rice soup. He did this so he could feed everybody in his family. I knew who gave my father that rice.

When I grew up, I had enough money to repay them for the rice. Now, every year after Christmas, I send some money to my village to feed the poor people in the village. I do that. I think I repay a debt of gratitude to those who helped my family. I do that every year.

We did not have enough rice to eat. All the Vietnamese people did not have enough rice to eat. The Japanese soldiers tried to destroy all of the rice. I can remember that most of the Vietnamese people did not have enough to eat.

In 1949, we came to the city. My father bought a shop. My mother started a small business. She established a café where she sold drinks and food to French soldiers. She got a lot of money. She was able to continue sending me and my sibling to the Catholic private school. The tuition was very high there.

At this time, The French established the Vietnam Government. Emperor Bao-Dai was the head of the Vietnam Nation at that time. He was Vietnamese. In the city, the government was controlled by Bao-Dai and the French. Surrounding areas were controlled by the Viet Minh. This is the name of the front of several political parties who were against the French. They were trying to get the French out of Vietnam. They included non-communist and communist parties who fought against the French. The neighborhood I lived in was controlled by Viet Minh during the night.

In the daytime, the national government controlled the neighborhood. My house was not very far from the Catholic school, so I walked to school. Every morning, when I came out of the house, I saw at least one dead person killed by the Viet Minh. I was a child. Almost every night, in the middle of the night, I would hear guns being fired by the Viet Minh. They used terrorism to scare people. It was bad. Very, very terrible.

The French had a secret organization called Surete Federale. They would come into your house and search anytime they wanted to. Anytime. Some nights, they would come to my house and take one of my relatives with them. They would keep them in jail for weeks. They would take my relatives and then bring them back. They suspected that my relatives had a relationship with the Viet Minh. It was very terrible. They would question them. They never took my father. They took my uncles.

I need to tell you this. I had an uncle who left our house in 1947. The French had returned to reoccupy my country. He joined the Vietminh to fight the French. He is the uncle that I loved most. So, when he disappeared, I suffered a lot. My suffering lasted for most of my young life. He was about ten years older than I am. He loved me very much. I remember my father had a bicycle. A bicycle was a big property in those days. It was a wonderful thing to have. It was very expensive. Every day, my uncle would take me to the sea. We rode together on the bicycle. He taught me how to read and write. If I wanted anything he had, he would give it to me. So, when he disappeared, I felt like I lost something. It caused me a lot of emotional stress.

He died during the Vietnam War. He disappeared when he followed the Viet Minh. I think he was not a Communist. Most Vietnamese people at that time tried to fight against the French colonists. I had one uncle killed during the French occupation and one during the United States occupation.

My View of United States Involvement in the Vietnam War

In 1954, the Vietnamese in the north became Communists. At this time, about a million people moved to South Vietnam to escape Communist rule. These poor people brought the habit of eating dogs with them. We lived in Hue then. My family had a peaceful time. I had a wonderful time with my family until 1954.

In 1954 the French were defeated in the Dien Bien Phu Battle. The French lost the War. According to the Geneva Accord, Vietnam was divided into two parts, North and South. One of the clauses of the Accord specified that general elections would be held in 1956 so that the people could choose the head of the government. So, the people could live in a democracy. Both sections were to unify.

The people were to choose who would be the head of the government. South Vietnam and the United States did not want a general election. They knew that the South would lose. All of Vietnam would then become Communists.

I would like to tell you that I think that the Vietnam War is something related to the consequences of World War II. After World War II, the Communists occupied Eastern Europe. They tried to conquer the rest of Europe. In Asia, the Chinese attempted to conquer all of Southeast Asia. Southeast Asia, to me, was a very important location for survival. This was a region mostly populated after China. Indonesia was the second most populated country after the War.

Most of the countries in that region were very poor. It would have been easy for the Communists to rule. They could have made the people believe that their lives would be better under Communist rule. I think that is the reason that the United States of America became involved in that War.

When the communists took over China in 1949, they tried to conquer all of the countries in Southeast Asia, even down to New Zealand and Australia. Vietnam is significant strategically in that region. In the Fourteenth Century, you must remember that the Mongols conquered most of that region from east to west. But they could not conquer Southeast Asia. It was difficult when they tried to conquer the Vietnamese people. They were defeated by the Vietnamese people before they could reach the other countries. Not just because the Vietnamese were good fighters but because of the terrain, the mountains.

If the United States of America had not been involved in the Vietnam War, Southeast Asia would have fallen into the hands of the Communists. I have always imagined Vietnam as a bridge that links China to Southeast Asia. You can see the shape of Vietnam. It has a long coast stretching from China to the South, about 1,500 miles. This is on the way from the Indian Ocean to the Pacific Ocean and on to North America. Vietnam is like a post to control the whole area.

I think the United States came to Vietnam to stop the possible invasion of China. Also, Vietnam has a very good bay. It's called Cam Ranh Bay. It is a wonderful bay because it looks like a great lake. It is a big lake. The water is very calm. From the sea, the entrance to the bay is like a gate. There are mountains on both sides of the opening. It is quite vast. During the War, the United States established a very important naval base there. I will talk with you later about the Cam Ranh Bay and why it is so important to the War and the safety of the United States.

The Vietnam War caused a controversy among the American people. When I came here, many people did not know why they sent their children to fight over there. It was very important for the Americans to come and fight. There were objectives to reach.

Politically, government leaders do not do things for the intent of other countries. They do things for the intent of their own country. The United States of America became involved in the Vietnam War not because the United States was afraid that the Vietnamese people would suffer from the Communists. The United States did it for their safety.

The involvement of the United States of America in the Vietnam War was a necessity. I believe in the domino theory. I think the United States was right to become involved in the War. If the Communists had conquered Vietnam, all the rest of the Southeast Asian countries would have fallen to the Communists. The people in this region were very poor. When the poor people first heard about Communism, they liked it. It seemed idealistic. But it is not.

When I was young, it seemed good in theory. When I went to law school, I learned about politics. I learned about the economy. Before, I had not believed in the economy.

The economics of Communism is not good. It is not good at all. When I studied economics, I learned that Communism is not good. It does not bring prosperity to the country. It kills motivation for the people to work. When you work, you expect some benefits to come to you. This does not happen in a Communist country. People under Communism's rule become poorer and poorer. The Government officials benefit. Not the ordinary people.

It is obvious. You can compare the situation of South and North Korea. South and North Vietnam. Cuba. In South Korea, the people have a very high standard of living. In the North, they don't even have enough food to eat. I am so confident to say that wherever the Communists go, they bring with them poverty and oppression to the people. That is right. Most ordinary people do not like Communism.

TRUC TRAN: My Story of a District Attorney in War

I believe in the Domino Theory. The involvement of the United States in Vietnam was a necessity. If the United States had not been involved, Southeast Asia would have fallen into the hands of the Communists. If all these countries had fallen into the hands of the Communists, it would have been a menace to the western part of the United States. If the American children had not gone to War in Vietnam, they would have later been fighting in the western part of the United States.

The second reason I want to advocate that the involvement of the United States in the Vietnam War was a necessity is because, during the Cold War with Russia, Vietnam, as a country, was very important because of its location. Russia has a very important naval base in Vladivostok. So, if the Communists had conquered Vietnam, they would have been able to use Cam Ranh Bay. This would have been a menace to the United States territory. Vietnam is strategically essential.

The countries surrounding Vietnam and the United States benefited economically from the War, as well. When the United States withdrew from Vietnam, all the countries in the region were economically and militarily strong enough to fight the Communists.

The United States decided to withdraw from Vietnam because of the unrest in the United States at that time. A lot of people protested the War. Another reason was that even if the Americans continued to help the South Vietnamese to win the War, the War would never end. Most of the North Vietnamese thought that they were doing the right thing, fighting against the South Vietnamese. When they fought against the South Vietnamese, they fought against the Americans.

The Americans came to Vietnam not to conquer the country but to help stop the invasion of the North into the South. The people did not understand. A lot of the South Vietnamese people thought that the North was right, as well.

During the Vietnam War, there were a lot of things happening to the South Vietnamese people. They lost relatives. They lost land. They were unable to farm what land they did have. There were many social problems. The country became two different cultures.

North and South Vietnam are separated by mountains. For thirty years, the North and South lived separately. The North Vietnamese people knew nothing about the South Vietnamese. The North thought that they were in a good situation because of Communism. The South had a much higher living standard, so they tried to fight.

I think that if the United States continued to drop bombs in the North, North Vietnam would have slowed down. But the Americans did not want to do that. They did not want to get China

TRUC TRAN: My Story of a District Attorney in War

into the War.

I want to tell you another very important thing. If you remember, President Tito (of Yugoslavia) and President of China were in 1968. Before that time, the United States had to face two enemies. The Russian and the Chinese. But after President Nixon went to China, China and the United States had a secret agreement. It was wise to do that. It is better to eliminate one enemy in case the two enemies were to become friendly. At that time, there was a conflict in ideology and thought between China and Russia. So, the Americans took advantage of the situation.

The United States became involved in the Vietnam War to prevent China from conquering all of Southeast Asia. Now, the United States had an agreement with China. That was a good time for the United States to withdraw from Vietnam. That is the reason.

I would like to emphasize the reason why the United States did not help South Vietnam to win the War before withdrawing. Because that could not happen. The War would not end. More civilians, especially ordinary people, would have fought to get the Americans out of their country. They did not know that they were the tools of the Chinese Communists. The Chinese Communists were using them to conquer themselves for Communist China.

So, the War would never end. And if the Americans withdrew from the Vietnam War, the consequence would be the collapse of South Vietnam. Everybody knew that. We lost the War in 1975.

If you understand what I am telling you, you can understand the involvement of the United States in the Korean War. If the Communists had been able to control South Korea, the ocean fleet could have managed to get to the West side of the United States. It was very important strategically.

If we lost the Vietnam War, the USSR could use Cam Ranh Bay as a naval base. Thailand is not a Communist country. Cambodia is a Communist country. Cambodia fell into the hands of the Communists two or three months before Vietnam and Laos.

My View of Communism

Now I say we lost the War, and I will tell you what is in the future and why and why not. Presently, the North and South are unified. All of the people of both parts of the country never understood what happened to one another because the majority of the South Vietnamese, especially the people in the country, live in the countryside. If the American had tried to help the South Vietnamese win the War, the War would not ever end. People would keep coming to fight the United States. It would never have ended.

Another thing is that if the War had ended, how much money and resources could the United States invest in Vietnam to help or rebuild. The United States looked like the enemy trying to take over the country.

The objective of the United States' involvement in the Vietnam War was to stop the Communists in Vietnam. I want to talk about all around the world and what the American Government tried to do at that time. They wanted to make Communism disappear from around the world. And if they let Vietnam fall into the hands of the North Vietnamese, all the Vietnamese would know what Communism is. They would find out what would happen to them. All the Vietnamese people do not like Communism, but they could not overthrow the Communists. The Communists rule the country like the police, with a gun. The people can do nothing.

Another thing is that this is an economic rule, a social problem that comes from the economics rule. It happens everywhere. That is what I noticed. For example, when the United States troops came to Vietnam, the Vietnamese society became worse because of bribery and corruption. When the United States came to Vietnam, a lot of changes occurred. Before they arrived, there was a class with a lot of money who had a good living standard. Civil servants, the high-ranking officers in the army, had a lot of money. And most of the ordinary people did not have enough money to eat. So, there is a different class structure now.

When the United States troops arrived, a lot of people worked for the Americans. Americans paid a lot of money. So, a lot of money went to the ordinary people. And if they had money, they had a tendency to buy things. In a country where the economy is not the same, they make a difference in the balance of supply and demand. You know the rule. If the demand is high and the supply is not. The price rises. That happened in Vietnam. They do not have enough merchandise to provide to the consumer.

I want you to understand this. This is very important. During the War, the economy depended on merchandise for use in the surrounding cities. They cannot do that if the economy cannot provide enough merchandise and good for the people. Only a minority of the people had enough money to buy merchandise. But the majority of people could not afford to buy things. So, the balance of demand and supply is unstable.

When the American troops and a mass of money went to the ordinary people, the high-ranking officials and the civil servants received a fixed salary. That means their salary did not rise. The ordinary people had a lot of cash money. They had the chance to go shopping. If they had a lot of money to buy merchandise, the price of the merchandise rose. They were reducing the supply. At the same time, the civil servants and high-ranking officers' salaries did not rise, so they did not have enough money to get things. That was the source of corruption. That happened terribly during the South Vietnamese War.

That also happened after the Communists won the war. The living standard between the South and the North was very different. So, when the North came to the South, this same thing happened after 1975. If the Communists say that everything they have done is for the poor people, the laborers, it is not true in Vietnam right now. The poor people are getting poorer and poorer. The high-ranking officials are becoming richer and richer.

I would like to tell you this so you can understand Communism. When the Russians occupied Eastern Europe, they tried to control all of the colonies. One of the countries opposed this and tried to resist them and it was Yugoslavia. The president then was Tito. In 1957, I think. In the 1950s, I found a book that was very interesting to me. I decided to read it. The name of the book is The New Class. I am talking about who wrote this book. His name is Jilas. Jilas was the Vice-President of Tito. Tito tried to oppose Communist Russia. He let Jilas do everything to find out the faults of Communism. Jilas had permission now to read any books he wanted.

When he read books about Communism, he found out that if the Communists tried to overthrow a government just because the ruler usually exploited the people and took everything out of their pockets, this situation made the country poor and made people miserable. For this reason, they tried to fight against the Communists.

After the Communists came to power, a new class rose. They tried to get the money out of their pockets. They tried to get rich from the mass of poor people. It is not a big book. It is very easy to read. I think it should be a rule for everybody to read this book.

Now, I will talk about the Vietnam War. When the United States withdrew from Vietnam, the Communists reunited the country and look what has happened to the people. A new class has risen in Vietnam. Even before I came over here. I know Vietnam has two classes. One was called Working Class and the other Working People. These two people became the main owners of society's means of products. Sadly, the communists came and created a new class of Red Capitalism. The ones benefiting are the ones in charge.

What did the United States want to do? I would like to tell you the objective of the United States foreign policy to make the Communists disappear. After 1975, the United States did nothing. The Communists collapsed. Now, the whole country is ruled by the Communists, but the rulers are not Communists anymore because they are rich. They are wealthy now. And the policy that is used to rule the country is not Communists anymore.

So, Vietnam is a Communist country, where the Communist Theory does not apply. The Vietnamese people live pretty much like other people in the world. They are restricted but they can do anything they want. They cannot leave the country. They are ruled under police security. The police can still come into your house anytime they want. If you cause no trouble, you are left alone.

Some people tell me that the United States lost the war. But they did not according to this. They lost the battle. But in the long run, the US won the war. That is what I tell many of my customers at the H.G. Hills Grocery Store about. The oppression is not as severe as it once was.

My wife can leave if she decides to leave, and I can go visit and return to the United States. I can come and go as I please, but if I decide to go back and live there, that would be a problem. They would try to bother me. Because they treated me just like an animal.

Truc Tran & Winston Vo

They searched my house any time of the day or night. Even at midnight, they just knocked at the door and searched my house.

What I have told you about the war is because of my logical thinking. I lived in the war, so I understand the reasons for it.

During the war, I did not fight.

My Elusive Nightmare

Vietnam is a very beautiful country. It has many beautiful cities. It is a peaceful country. I think it affected my emotional life. Many mountains and rivers can be seen there. I love my country. I was born and grew up in a natural beauty of Hue City, an ancient capital of Vietnam.

When my mother died in 1960, my youngest brother became my best friend. Everything I did with him. I slept with him on the same bed. I loved him so much; sometimes, I asked myself if I needed a wife. And if I got married, which one would I sleep with. He was a very, very good boy.

He was a scout boy. He could do everything. He could fix the door. He could help the people. Every day, he tried to do one thing good for his society. One morning, the Communists surrounded and occupied the area where we lived at my house. I heard them. My youngest brother and I were in the room casting. I heard the knock on the door, on the front door. I stood up and I saw through my window several Communist soldiers outside my window. They asked us to open the door.

My sister, the one who lives here in the United States, went and opened the door. When she answered the door, one soldier asked, "Where is Mr. Phuc?"

My name is Truc. They didn't call my name. They called for Mr. Phuc.

Someone called my name incorrectly. My sister was very smart.

She said, "Oh, yeah. My brother named, Fruc, Phuc is now in the Military Court. I have another brother whose name is Truc. He is here with me. The one you asked about is now in the Military Court."

They raised their voices and my sister pretended to cry. She led them far from the house. My other sister asked me to get out of the house through another door. I got out the side door.

When I jumped the fence to another house, I saw a young teenager with a grenade in his hand.

He yelled, "Where are you going? Why are you running?"

I didn't stop to talk with him. He could not run as fast as I could. So, I went into another house. I continued to go back to my house another way. Every morning, they came back. We knew that they would. My brother and I would sit somewhere, hiding behind something in the house. When I saw them enter my house, I would go out into another house. They would go and search the next house. I would wander around until I could come back to my house. I had to do this every day. They tried to catch me.

TRUC TRAN: My Story of a District Attorney in War

One day, my brother and I hid behind my friend's house. The soldier knocked on the door of my friend's house. They said they wanted to search his house because someone in his house had just shot them. But no one in the house had shot them.

I thought, now I am dead. Because there was no way to get out of that house. Then, my friend was a teacher at a very big high school. He talked with the Communists and said no one in there had shot them.

But you know what, once they had captured the city, the young people in the neighborhood would shoot at the United States helicopters every time they saw one pass over. All the teenagers had guns in their hands because they wanted to shoot. When they passed the house where we were, someone shot. The soldiers thought that someone in the house tried to shoot them. But after my friend talked with them, they decided it was nothing. I was very lucky.

I stayed with these boys for fourteen days after the capture of my area. Soon, we found out that we had nothing to eat. One of my aunts tried to go to another relative's house to get some rice to eat. When she stepped outside, she was shot by an American soldier. A lot of people brought her to my house. Because of her injury, a lot of people tried to come to help her. It became a target for the U.S. Fighter planes. The people in the street tried to fight the mortar shell. During the fight, my brother was killed. I lost my aunt and my brother.

When he was shot, I was hiding in another house. The Communists were trying to catch me. When I heard that he was shot, I didn't care about myself. I came out to take him to the Pagoda, the Buddhist Temple, to ask people to help. But he died before dark. He was fourteen years old. I was so desperate. I did not want to live. My younger brother was fourteen and in the eighth grade when he died. He was very smart. He knew everything.

When he was alive, he just wanted a knife. You know, the Scout Boys only wanted to have a knife to have when he went to camp and play in the jungle. When the United States expelled the Communists from the city, I was wondering on the street. And I saw it. The knife that my brother wanted. I tried to pick it up. But then I thought, why? I did not. Oh, I cried. I believe that is the reason why I decided to get married when I saw my wife.

My Wife

I was very, very sad because I had nothing to make me want to live. I lost my mother. I lost my little brother. I had no girlfriends. I was 26 years old. Then I met my wife.

I remember that year. I was at home.

A cousin of mine came and asked me, "Please come with me to see a beautiful girl."

I thought, "Yeah, that's okay!" I saw my wife.

I married her not because of her beauty but because of her good behavior. The manner in which she treated people so well. She was a very nice, kind, and loving person. That is why I decided to marry her.

We got married in 1970. She was a teacher in a Pedagogy School. She was born in 1945. I went with my cousin the first night I went to her house. After that, I came and talked with her alone. At that time in Vietnam, we were not allowed to go out together until we became engaged. That was the culture.

One year later, we were engaged. And one year after the engagement, we got married. I asked the father's permission to marry her. It was a very complicated procedure to get married. We married in a Confucius ceremony.

My Education

I would like to start with after I graduated from law school. I have told you that I graduated from law school in May 1964. I went into the Army in November of 1964. After spending nearly one year in infantry school, I became an Aspirant. Before becoming a Second Lieutenant, you must be an Aspirant. After that, they appointed me to work as a clerk in the Military Court in Hue, the city where I was born.

In one year, I was promoted to Second Lieutenant and appointed to be a Military Prosecutor in the court. That was a very quick promotion because of my abilities. Six months later, I was promoted to Prosecutor. After that, I worked for the Military Court in Hue and then the Military Court in Da Nang as a Military Prosecutor.

I learned French, so two years before I came to the United States in 1993, I began to learn to speak English. So, I don't know much of the Military vocabulary in English. But I know all the French.

My job over there was to prosecute all the people who were linked with the Communists. If they came to the South to cause trouble, I was to put them in prison. There was a big prison in the province. This is where the convicted felons were placed. This is not the same type of prison I was placed in.

TRUC TRAN: My Story of a District Attorney in War

In Communist countries, they never call the facility a prison or a jail. They call them Re-Education Camps. All Re-Education Camps were established deep in the jungle. Prisoners were sent to the Re-Education Camps in the North and the South for policy and philosophy because, according to Criminology, we sometimes consider that someone who commits a crime does it not by his fault. Someone does that because of the influence of society upon him. Something in society caused him to want to do that. Born has something bad in their genes. In my family, I have two nephews. They receive the same education and eat the same food but one loves cats and the other one does not. That is not the child's fault.

Another reason is something in his genes makes him hate cats. So, according to criminology, sometimes a criminal is not responsible for his actions. Society doesn't need to punish this person. It is not the fault of the criminal that he committed the crime. So, they try to isolate them so that he or she does not bother society. Then, they are re-educated so that they can become a good citizen.

The criminal is taught to see why what he did was wrong. So maybe he will not do it again. He doesn't need to be punished. I learned criminology when I was in law school. I don't know what they think about it in the United States. The Communist way is to Re-Educate criminals, but in reality, they do not. They are mean to everybody.

I received my law degree in the summer of 1964. On November 11, I went to the Army according to the law. I was placed in the Infantry School where, after training, I became a Second Lieutenant. After that, I was assigned to work as a village prosecutor. There, I prosecuted the Communists and the people who were South Vietnamese but supported the Communists. I did not carry a gun. I was not in the infantry.

My sister in Vietnam was not able to visit me because her husband had been injured during the war. He got out of the Army before the war ended. He went to Law School and finished the second year in 1975. He did not complete his last classes. My brother-in-law, who is here now, the same as I, came over here as a refugee because of the international intervention, according to the United States. They helped us come over here. They did not help me for political reasons but for humanitarian reasons.

In 1964, after earning a law degree and working for the Army, I came back to work in a military court in Hue for two or three years. In 1968, North Vietnam launched a general attack on the cities in South Vietnam. They killed a lot of people. They attached on foot with hand weapons. They occupied the city and killed millions. They surprised the people. They took advantage of people who were celebrating the Lunar New Year at that time of year all over the city. When I think of that, I am full of so much anguish because I was a victim in that.

TRUC TRAN: My Story of a District Attorney in War

I was an Army Prosecutor in the Hue-Danang Military Courts from 1966 to 1969. I ran into the Ministry of Justice. They needed some judges, so they organized an exam. I took the test. I was chosen one among thirty people to be a judge.

In 1970, I was appointed an Attache au Parquet, Hue Court. In the French law system, this means someone who gets ready to spend two years as an apprentice to become a judge.

In 1971, I was appointed as the District Attorney in the Qui Nhon Court in Hue. Hue is a higher judicial system. The Vietnam judicial system is divided into tribunal classes: First, Second and Third. Qui Nhon is a very big city. It was a significant city. At that time, the Hue and Saigon courts were classified as the highest class, not like the US Supreme Court. There were two appeal courts. One in Saigon and one in Hue.

There were a lot of foreign students stationed there. A lot of allies were stationed there. Koreans, Thailand, the United States, and Australian troops were stationed there. There were a lot of problems in this city.

After a long time, they appointed me to the highest position of District Attorney in this area. They appointed me because of the recommendation of the Attorney General. According to the French Law system, the head of state appoints the judges and the district attorneys, not like here in the United States. This was a very important position. According to the French legal system, the District Attorney position is more important than the judge. The District Attorney in the French law system has the responsibility to keep everything in society in order.

Procureur de la Appeal Republic was my title. If you know the meaning of the title, you may understand how important the District Attorney was in French law. A long time ago, when the King was very busy, he would appoint someone to do a job for him. So, he called him Procureur de Roi. When we don't have kings anymore, and we become a republic, they call them Procureur de la Appeal Republic. You can imagine how important this position is. In the province, it is higher than the government. I could arrest anyone.

I read the Bible a lot. I used to be a student in a Catholic school. When I was there, I went to the --, a small church, twice a day. I never was baptized a Catholic. I studied the Bible almost one hour every day when I attended Catholic high school.

Ecole Pellerin was the first Catholic school I attended. When I was in Secondary School, I went to another Catholic School established by the Fathers of the Mission Etrangere de Paris. It was the best school in Hue City. I got a good education. I am lucky to have gotten a good education.

I had to take an entrance exam to attend this school. I think one of the Vietnamese priests here in Nashville comes from the same school. Father Peter. When I was young, I attended Mass. But I don't, now.

When I grew up and learned more about science, I drifted more and more away from the Catholic Church. Especially after I studied astrology. When I investigated the Bible and the Old Testament, I learned about science. I believed that the Old Testament is a series of Fairy Tales. I believe it is a History of man. The relationship I now have with Christianity is the Bible, the Old and New Testament. I revere the Bible as a form of philosophy. Not theology.

If you live in compliance with the Bible, you will be a good person. When I was in prison for nine years, I prayed almost every night. But day by day, it did not solve any problems for me or for my family. One day, a friend of mine who was a member of the -- in Vietnam gave me a Buddhist Book about Zen Meditation. First, I just wanted to find out what information was in the book. But more and more, I learned the book was no different from the Bible.

I think that meditation saved me when I was in prison. That is why I think I survived the psychological trauma. Or the "re-education camps." A nice way to refer to a concentration camp is "re-education camp." "We're going to re-teach you everything. You live the way we want you to live."

Truc Tran & Winston Vo

My Incarceration

They tried to kill us. All of us. But they could not do that because of a relationship with the outside world. If they killed us, they would have problems with other countries. So, they could not. So, they went and put us in prison. They forced us to work hard, physical labor, and gave us very little to eat.

We built the prison. They didn't have to spend any money. We grew vegetables, rice, and food to feed the people who were holding us prisoner. When I entered the prison, I weighed about 160 pounds. When I was in prison in the South, my family gave me food. When they sent me to prison in the North, my weight dropped to about 100 pounds.

I lost 60 pounds. I did not have enough energy to stand up. Because of the international intervention, they allowed our family to provide us with food. I had no family in the North, but our family went from the South to the North to feed me.

I remember one winter it was very cold. I was in prison. A friend of mine told me, "Hey, your father is here!"

But they did not want to let me see my father. The reason was I was not a good prisoner. I usually opposed them and said bad things to them. I was not allowed to see my father. But they allowed him to leave food for me. When I learned that they did not allow my father to see me, I was crazy. I said bad things to them.

When I did that, I only said it to my roommate in the room. But someone reported it to the prison official. The next day, the Communist Cadre came and asked me about my family. How often have I received letters from my family and everything else related to this issue?

I had to talk about what I had said. They said they heard that I had said ugly things about the Communist Party.

"You said ugly things about us. Why?" they asked me.

I said, "What do you mean ugly? I did not say ugly things. I said the truth." I did say the truth.

The Communist Cadres usually told us that they loved us. That they were trying to re-educate us. But the truth is not that. They did it differently. Not the same way others did.

They said, "You are not a good prisoner. According to the rule of the prison, you are not allowed to see your family."

I said, "That's okay! But if I am not a good prisoner, I cannot see my family. What about my father? He did nothing wrong, so that you did not allow him to see his son. Those are two different things."

They say, "Did you know that your father came over here without any permit paper?"

We had to build our jail. We had to work to grow food to feed ourselves, the Warden, and the jail guards. They didn't have to spend anything on us. We had to do everything... and right now.

The first time I went to a Re-Education Camp in Long Thanh, they imprisoned me with juvenile criminals. Every morning, they spoke in the announcement speakers to the juveniles, telling them how to be better citizens.

After that, the Guards abused them. They would beat them terribly. When we witnessed that, all the former regime officials protested. It was terrible. One juvenile stood in the center of four guards. One would hit the boy. The boy would fall into another guard's area, and that guard would hit him, and so on and so on. They kept taking turns beating on him, just like a bag of sand. Oh, it was terrible.

In Vietnam, the people usually say, "Don't believe what the Communists say. Watch what they do!"

Every morning, we would wake up at 5:00 am and do exercises together. At 6:00 am, we would gather in the large outside yard area to go to the field to work. We would work all day long from Sun up to Sun down.

TRUC TRAN: My Story of a District Attorney in War

We would stop for lunch. We would eat in the field. We would come back to the jail before dark. They did not want us out after dark for fear that we would escape. We would eat dinner.

After dinner, we had to sit down around in groups of ten. We would talk about what we had done during the day. We were told to fault and criticize one another. Sometimes, we would argue until midnight. We would then go to bed and get up again at 5:00 am in the morning.

That is the way they wanted us to do. To criticize each other. They didn't want us to think about anything positive. They wanted us to be negative thinkers. Another thing is that they gave us very little to eat. Almost all the times of the day, we would think about food. Wanting food. Nothing else. So, it was terrible. It was hard to remain a gentleman through difficult times.

I remember one of my friends, whose name is Lun Hoang. He used to be a District Attorney in Dalat. He was very funny. He was always optimistic. One day, he sent a letter to his wife.

He asked her, "Please sell my watch and send me the money!"

One day, he received a lot of money from her, 100 Dong. This was a lot of money at that time. Two days later... when we went to work in the fields, they would not allow us to wear shoes. Just bare feet. Even in the winter when it was very cold. No shoes. He told one of the guards that his feet hurt. He needed to wear shoes because his feet hurt.

One morning, around 11:00 am, he disappeared with his shoes on. When he was on the border between China and Vietnam, he was arrested. They tied him just like a pig and brought him back to the prison. Then, right at that time, they called me and accused me of helping him to escape. They put me in a cell for three days.

I said, "I did not. Because if I had prepared for him to escape, I would have escaped with him."

At the same time, they pressed my friend to tell them that I had helped him escape.

My friend said, "No, he did not help me escape. What you want to know is the truth. And I can say the truth only. He did not help me at all."

I was released from the cell and put back to work in the field.

Everything that happened in the jail was blamed on me. They said I was the one who organized anything that went wrong. I was the worst inmate in the jail.

One day, they called me to the office and told me, you know that you cannot do anything bad to this jail. Because if you do that, your inmate will tell us what you did. It was their effort in Re-Education.

I said, "No, I have not done anything. Because the South Vietnamese have a very big army, they have a naval force; we have a lot of planes. But we did not win the war. What can I do if I have nothing in my hand?"

And he said that somebody told him that I tried to do something.

I said, "I'm not crazy"

You know that prison is a very small society where we especially miss a lot of things. We're poor. All we had every day was suffering, half starving. So, it is easy to have conflict often between us, because the prison made everyone so unhappy.

Truc Tran & Winston Vo

My First Attempt at Re-Location

In March 1975, my family and I flew to the South because of the war. The South was ready for the Communist attacks. I think that this is important. I want everybody to know about the days approaching the end of the Vietnam War.

April 30, 1975, the last day of the war. I want to begin with this. At that time, everybody, and even now, the people living here in the United States, believed what the BBC Radio and the VOA Radio said to be the gospel truth. They believed that. Almost every day and every evening, people would stop doing things and turn on the radio to listen to the BBC and the VOA. Why did they believe what was broadcasted?

I remember in 1962-1963, there was a movement to overthrow the first president of Vietnam. His name was Ngo Dinh Diem. He and his family were Catholic. Eighty to eighty-five percent of Vietnamese are non-Catholic. The Communists don't like Catholics.

There was a movement to overthrow him. Every day, people needed to know what happened. Only the BBC and the VOA told the truth about this. We had the habit of listening to the BBC. I still have that habit today.

TRUC TRAN: My Story of a District Attorney in War

I want you to know how important the BBC and the VOA radio were to the Vietnamese people at that time. When the war was closer to the end, the war was terrible. We usually listened to the BBC Radio. One day, BBC Radio reported that two or three groups, governed by a General (Division), were coming.

Everybody tried to flee the South. I didn't flee when I learned about this. As experience had shown me, I knew that when the United States officials left, that is when I should leave. I was okay as long as the United States was still here. I did not leave when I listened to the BBC about the information. I contacted someone who watched the United States base to see if they were still there or not. I began to use my car to take my wife, my daughter, and me to Da Nang.

Two or three days later, while I was in Da Nang, the Communist entered the city (Hue). They captured the city without a fight. When everybody heard that the Communist had entered the city, everybody tried to flee to the South. But I did not, because I was watching the United States base. I was an important official in the city, so I had responsibility. I felt safe as long as the Americans were there. Two or three days before the Communist came. The same thing happened in Da Nang and other cities. I want to let you know that. The story I just told you, made me think that Americans wanted to accelerate the fall of South Vietnam. The BBC Radio said that the Communist units had surrounded the cities. Everybody tried to flee south. Hue was not captured by the Communist until three or four days later.

I believe that the VOA and the BBC took information from the Intelligence. The radio told the people that the Communist had surrounded the city before it came to it so that they could evacuate. Everywhere, people were evacuating. They used every means of transportation to leave. It was terrible, by car, on foot, by bicycle, by motor bicycle. There were people dying alongside the road. It was terrible. A lot of people died.

When I was in Da Nang, the BBC and the VOA said that the Communist would capture Cam Ranh Bay in one or two days. Everybody tried to get out. My wife, my daughter, who was three months old, and I, my family, spent two nights on the beach to get a boat. We failed to get one. Then we decided to commit suicide. I would kill my daughter, then my wife, and then myself.

At first, my wife agreed with that, but then she said, "No!"

When I took out my pistol, she said, "No, I don't want that."

We left the beach and went to an abandoned house.

One morning, I was very desperate. I waited for the Communist to come, capture, and kill me. I listened to Ranh Lam, a friend of mine who was an attorney who worked for the Americans.

TRUC TRAN: My Story of a District Attorney in War

He said, "Oh, there is an army boat that is going to leave for the South,"

Then I was very happy. Early in the morning, nobody but the Vietnamese Marines was shooting. This was very dangerous. But I didn't care about this. My friend took his bicycle and used his car to bring me back to my house to take my wife and daughter. But when we reached the place where we expected a boat to be waiting for us, it had just left. It was right in front of us. I was very desperate.

At that time, I had a referral note in my pocket, a note from a cousin of my wife. He was a Colonel in the Vietnamese Navy. The note was to be taken to the Naval Commander in Da Nang to help us. My friend took my family to the Vietnam Naval Base. When he saw the Communist, he said he could not help us. He did not have any authority to help us.

Suddenly, out of nowhere, we saw a gate with many people trying to enter. The naval soldiers were trying to stop them. When we got there, my wife cried. I showed one of the soldiers the note from my wife's cousin, and he let us come in. We tried to find a boat. I saw a Navy First Lieutenant. When he saw me, he saluted me.

He said, "Teacher, do you remember me?"

I did not remember him.

He asked me, "Where are you going?"

I said, "I am going to get a boat so that I can go South."

He said, "Me, too!"

We walked along the riverside. Someone in a Navy boat called out to me, a friend that I used to play tennis with me. He tried to help us get in a small boat. All four of us.

About a hundred miles into the water, we ran out of gas. Fortunately, we saw a Vietnamese Naval Destroyer. The Naval officer in my boat signaled to the Destroyer by light that we were out of gas. The Destroyer allowed us to come on board.

The boat was so big that we had to use a rope ladder to climb aboard. I was afraid to let my wife and my daughter go up there. My wife was very weak. She was very sick. The Navy First Lieutenant told me he would help her.

She went up the ladder with him behind her in case she should fall. He could catch her. Finally, she made it onto the boat. Holding one hand on the rope ladder and my baby in the other, I climbed the rope. It was so hard.

We spent one day and a half going from one boat to another. Then we were very hungry. When we got on the boat, I looked for the kitchen. For the first time in my daughter's life, she ate soup. We tried to give her a meal with carrots or other vegetables. Not the stuff that the soldiers eat.

TRUC TRAN: My Story of a District Attorney in War

We landed in Cam Ranh Bay. I was unfamiliar with the city because this was my first time there. I just wandered around. A lot of the Vietnamese Marines were robbing people, trying to get money. One of them, I heard about later when I was in prison.

I saw a friend of mine who was a Marine Captain. We were friends when we were in the Infantry School. After that, when I was in prison, he told my brother, that this man tried to rob me because they knew that I was a District Attorney. The Captain told him not to do that because he was my friend.

I tried to find out who was the police chief in Cam Ranh Bay. That night was terrible. The Marines were looting and shooting everywhere and trying to injure the Police Chief. One Marine was shot right in the house of the Police Chief. I believe he was killed. The Police Chief had tried to keep the city calm. Early in the morning, we got a jeep, and we went to Cam Ranh City.

On the way to Cam Ranh, we saw a lot of people from Cam Ranh going South because the BBC and the VOA had warned them the city was occupied by the Communist. They were fleeing, but I was going. I could not find anyone I knew, even the Province Chief. I had to go back to Cam Ranh Bay.

We tried to catch another boat going South. And then something happened. The VOA and the BBC said something about them trying to warn us. We spent about four or five days waiting for another boat. Finally, I got to onboard an American Merchant boat named Pioneer. You know that to get to the Pioneer, we had to get on board a flat bottom boat, an infantry carrier.

When we reached the Pioneer to go on board, it was very, very high. They dropped a rope basket that is used to pick up merchandise off the dock and put it on board.

When they dropped the basket, people rushed to be the first ones in the basket. I pushed my wife to get inside. I got into the next net that was dropped, one hand on the net and one holding my baby, I climbed in. We spent one or two days reaching our destination.

The situation was very bad in Saigon. They did not allow us to land there. They asked us to go to an island (Phu Quoc) very far from Saigon. When I was there. I looked for a refugee camp.

A Captain came up to me and asked me, "What are you doing?"

I said, "I just got off this boat."

He invited me to stay at his house. I used his telephone to call the Ministry of Justice. They sent people to come and get me to return back to Saigon.

If I did not have the phone number to call the Ministry of Justice, I would have been in the United States on the first day after

TRUC TRAN: My Story of a District Attorney in War

this. Most people, refugees, got on board a Naval boat to go to Guam and then to the United States of America. I went on to Saigon to look for help.

When I got to Saigon, I saw somebody who told me about the collapse of the South Vietnamese Government. I did not have any idea about this. My wife could not go with me because of her weakness. I didn't want to leave her and our baby. One morning, the President of the South Vietnamese declared surrender.

A friend of mine, who got on a boat, is now in Montreal, Canada. He is very rich now.

He came to my house and said, "Let's go."

I saw his car in front of my house.

"You need to leave, or they'll kill you."

I intended to leave, but when I left my house, the first thing I saw was my father. It was very hot. So hot that he did not wear a shirt. And I saw the wrinkles on his face and body. I tried to get out, but when I got out of the door, I saw my wife with our baby in her hands. She was sitting on the bench. She was very sad. I told my friend, I'm not leaving. I couldn't go.

My friend went to Guam. When he reached Guam, he chose to go to Montreal, Canada, because he spoke French. He did not speak English. If I had gone with him, I would have chosen to go to Canada as well, because I speak French. I could not speak English then, either. I will tell you how I learned to speak it.

I waited for them to arrest me, but they did not arrest me. They did not arrest me. One day, I listened to the radio. An announcement was made stating that the officials of the Ancient Regime, of the Saigon Regime, needed to show up at the high school, Gia Long High School, with enough money to eat for thirty days for the Re-Education camp.

Everybody thought, "Oh, we are lucky they didn't kill us."

They asked us to go for thirty days to learn how to live in a new society. Everybody was happy. When we went in, they sent us to an orphanage called Long Thanh. It's about sixty kilometers from Saigon. We were kept there. Day by day, we hoped they would release us after thirty days, but they did not. This is when I began my nine-year term as a Prisoner of War. Thirty days turned into nine years.

TRUC TRAN: My Story of a District Attorney in War

My Nine Years as a Prisoner of War

After one year, they tried to select the people that they thought were dangerous for the Regime. They sent them to the North. I was one of those. During this time, my wife went to Hue to continue her job as a teacher. She worked and took care of our daughter. One year after showing up at meet up concentration (Saigon), they sent me to the North.

They told us, "Now you are being sent to a comfortable place for your re-education."

When we got in line to get on the truck, they began to cuff and chain our hands, two men together. A friend of mine cried. He never realized that one day, he would be in chains. He used to be the Vice Mayor of --.

I told him, "Don't worry. They are the winners, and we are the losers. We can do nothing about it. Just go with it."

They put us in a boat that they used to transport charcoal. They put us in a place where they stowed charcoal. We got dirty, and black. Then, they covered the opening so that we were enclosed in a box. I don't remember exactly. It seems it took us two or three days to reach the North.

They put a bucket right in the center of the storage area. Everybody used it, there, to eliminate. Every morning, they used a rope to pull it up and emptied it into the sea. Everyday. While we were on the ship, we were fed. I don't remember what, but we were fed enough. We did not have much water, though. But that was good for us because we did not have to urinate as often.

One morning, it felt like the boat stopped. They asked one of my friends to go up to empty the waste bucket.

When he came back, he said, "It's Hai Phong! I believe it is Hai Phong Port!"

Hai Phong is very important in the North. We thought we would be going to an important place. (Why is this place important?)

We landed in Hai Phong Port. They put us on a bus. They covered the windows so that we could not see out or know where we were going. After a long time of riding, they stopped. I don't remember what for. A lot of people were working in that area. They rushed to the bus to look at us. To see us. The police, escorting us, tried to keep them away.

But someone said, "Let me see! The people who eat human meat."

They used that means of propaganda to keep people from talking to us. They wanted the people to be afraid of us.

TRUC TRAN: My Story of a District Attorney in War

People tried to approach our bus to see us. A friend of mine stomped his foot hard on the floor of the bus. All the people ran away. They were afraid we were going to eat them. They took us to the Re-Education Camp.

We spent a long day because we landed on shore early in the morning and arrived at the prison camp that night. I remember the Phu Son Camp is in Bac Thai Province. It's a very poor province in the North. In the morning, we were there. The first day they feed us --. We did not complain. We could do anything about it. At about 1:00 pm, the ration of food declined.

One day, the Vietnamese talked to our battalion, or hut of prisoners, about what we needed to do. First, if we want to become re-educated men in the new society, we need to perform hard labor.

They put us in the field. We plowed the land just like a farmer. We did everything. They gave us prisoners clothes. Every pair of pants and every shirt had a sign that said "Prisoner" on them. They were blue.

We worked just like forced labor. We were forced labor. We worked all day in the sun, every day. Every morning when we left, we would leave them a can at the camp. Someone would fill the can with water. When we came back, we drank. While we worked in the fields, we were living out in the open. No tents. We sat under the shade of a tree. We had nowhere to live. We were just out in the jungle. At the end of the day, we would go back to the prison. We spent every day like that.

The prison was built like a house with rooms. About forty people stayed in one room. We lay down, side by side, to sleep at night. Just like you arrange sardines in a can. No mattresses. There were only forty prisoners on the floor.

There was one re-educator. That was one of their titles. His main job was to watch us. Learn what we think and watch what we do during the day. When we went to work in the field, usually, two guards with automatic weapons stayed with us.

We stayed there, in that prison, until 1979, when the Chinese attacked them. There was a conflict, a fight in North Vietnam, between China and Vietnam in 1979. They evacuated us to Thanh Hoa.

Thanh Hoa is a province noted for very bad air. It is not good for your health. A lot of precious kinds of trees grow there that release poisons into the air. I don't know how to explain. You could not touch it. It is a precious tree. It is very big and hard. Very precious.

Thanh Hoa is classified as the worst province of the North. There were many bugs, snakes, and mosquitoes. We had a mosquito net. They gave everyone one during the night when we slept.

TRUC TRAN: My Story of a District Attorney in War

While we were there, we heard the guards talking about trying to concentrate on locating all the former officials of the former regime. Some of our generals. Some people who used to be the leaders of the Saigon Regime. I heard that they were going to put all of us there.

Before we moved, there were a lot of South Vietnamese soldiers who were in the Special Forces who went to the North schools. They tried to complete things in the North. They would capture officials and put them in another camp. When the Chinese invaded, they moved our unit to their location.

When I moved there, the educator that I had been given told me to dig a hole right in the watershed to put human manure. He asked me to dig this hole to put our waste from the prisoners in. After some time, we would use the manure to grow vegetables. I was a headache person. I caused a lot of problems for the guards.

I said, "Why? When the rainy season comes, all the bacteria and viruses in the waste will go into the water supply and filter down to the villages in the lower countryside. The people will be infected."

At that time, dysentery was very bad.

I said, "I cannot do that. If I do that, the people in the village will be sick." When we argued about this, the guard said, "You always oppose our orders."

I said, "No! I do not."

Suddenly, I saw three or four people come out of the bushes. I knew that they were officials coming over to inspect me.

They asked, "What happened?"

I told them what I had said.

They said, "You are right. From now on, all of you have the right to participate in the management of the camp."

It was great. But I was thinking that they would try to keep all of us for life.

They did not say this, but that's what they meant.

"And if your family wants to come, they can."

That meant they planned to concentrate on the person and the family of the person who will be there for life. They might bring our families to stay here also.

On another day, they asked us to make a path to clear the forest. I found about ten houses while we were working. Several people went by us. They acted like they did not see us. As if we were not there. When I said something to them, they wouldn't speak.

A boy came by. I gave him a long knife that the Vietnamese had given us to cut the foliage for the path. I put the knife on the ground and left it there. The next day, when I came back, the knife was gone. (Did the boy approach you... how did you get to talk with him?)

The boy came to me. I asked him why he was here. He said that his family used to work for the French. In 1954, when the nation was divided, they refused to go to the South. So, they concentrated on the middle of the jungle. (Were they prisoners, too?) Some of them used to be surgeons in the French Army. They worked for the non-communist government. They told us that every two years, they resettled. (Who resettled them? Did they do this on their own, or because they were forced to?) What I learned from him gave me reason to believe that they were going to move my family here. They were going to isolate our families to be near us. I did not want that. Our children would become ignorant, just like an animal in the jungle or zoo. We were desperate, but there was no way to escape. I was in this camp until 1982.

In 1982, they sent us to another camp in the South that they called Z-30. It was in Long Khanh, about 100 km from North Saigon. The life there was better. Why they sent us there, I believe, was because of international pressure. Especially pressure from the United States of America. They had to leave.

The war ended in 1975. In 1982, they sent me to Z-30 camp. The life was better there. Our family could provide food for us.

Because we had food, we could bribe the jailers. That made our lives easy.

They were very poor. Lanterns, pens, they needed everything. They would let us have an easy life. They wouldn't bother us. We had to work in the field every day, but not as hard as before. And we could do fun things, like sing a song. We could do many things that we could not do before.

When I was young, I played the flute, not like a flute made here. It was made from bamboo. A Chinese flute. One night, I started playing it and they came and took it away from me. They confiscated it from me in the other prison.

Then, one day, they called my name and let me go out of the prison.

My Release from Prison

When I was released from the camp, they gave me some money for transportation from the camp to Saigon. I rode the bus. The amount of money they gave me was not enough to pay for the transportation from the camp to Saigon and then from Saigon to my house. I caught a person who gives rides on motorcycles. A lot of people use motorcycles to carry people where they want to go, like a taxi. I asked him to take me to my house. When I reached my house, my sister paid the driver. I had no more money.

When I was in front of my house, the first person I saw was my sister. My sister later lived with me. I bought a two-story house. The upper story was for my family and the lower floor was for my sister's family. Oh, she was so happy that she screamed. My wife came to the balcony and looked down. She saw me and tears came streaming down her face.

I stayed in my house for one day. On the next day, I had to show up at the police station to show them my release papers. According to the rule, I had to show up once a week to show a diary in which I wrote things that I did every day. According to the rules, if I need to go out of the South, I need to have permission.

One day I put in my diary that I went to a friend of mine's house in another district. It took about ten minutes on a motorcycle. The reason I went was to attend the --.

At the end of the week, when I showed them this, they said, "Why did you go somewhere else, you didn't get permission?"

I said, "No, I obeyed the rule. I only need to get permission when I go out of town."

He shouted at me. Then I said, "I'm sorry."

I told him, "The next time I go somewhere, I will come by the police station and get permission."

Then I gave him something. A Bic ballpoint pen. Oh, it was very precious then. It was made in the United States of America, of course. And after that, he was easy with me.

Every month, my sister and my father gave me some money so I could take the police to a restaurant. They did not bother me anymore. But you know, they were so ungrateful for what I did. Whenever I said I was going to take a policeman to lunch, he would gather all of his friends at work to go with us. He didn't care how much money I had to spend. That's the way they did it. So, life was better, but still, I was unable to do anything. I couldn't even work.

TRUC TRAN: My Story of a District Attorney in War

My father owned a house in Hue. After the war, it became a very good place for business. He made a lot of money. For example, my wife, who taught in public school, earned about 30 Dong per month, while my father made 84 Dong a day. So, he gave me a lot of money.

One of my brothers-in-law was released from Ham Tan Camp. He did not want to go back to Hue because the Communists there were very fanatical. Even though his wife lived there, he would not go. He lived in Saigon with me. He tried to make money. He learned to survey the market. He made a bag just like a school bag. He made a lot of money over there. I worked for him.

In 1988, the poverty of life after the war was terrible. People did not have enough food. The Communists had failed to make the economy better with their theory. The value of the money depreciated. They began to change the policy, just like they did in Russia. That means that they opened the door for Red Capitalism.

I got a job as an office manager in a private Vietnamese trading company. Trading was done inside Vietnam, not internationally. I bought about twenty shares from the company. I invested. I did not get any profit from this because they -- a lot.

They tried to get money from the company that owed them, but they didn't. I didn't make a lot of money. I did get the money I invested back.

Then, one day, a friend of mine from Australia sent me a note to introduce me to a businessman from Australia. That man wanted to do business in Vietnam. He appointed me a representative for his company. The name of the company is CMS Group (Commodity Management Services).

TRUC TRAN: My Story of a District Attorney in War

My Mercantile Adventure

I made a lot of American Dollars working for the Australians. Some people are making $10 to $20 a week and I'm making $200. I tried to help them to build up their business. Whatever they asked me to do, for example, to survey the needs of the market. They asked me to find merchandise so that they could get it to provide for another country. I did this perfectly. But what made me disappointed was that they did not do anything that I did.

They wanted to buy several tons of rice to send to Africa. I tried to make contact with the supplier. I would get everything they needed, and then, finally, they would not complete the transaction. Finally, they did nothing. When I do that, I get a bonus, so they did not want me to have that bonus.

A friend of mine, who is a lawyer, he introduced me to the Russin & Vecchi Law Firm. I worked for them as an attorney and translator. I translated the contracts from Vietnamese to English and versa, from French to English and versa.

I did research when they were writing contracts. I would look to see if the translation made sense or was correct. I took part in a lot of very important contracts. For example, a contract with Heineken Beer for a Japanese Company because they made a joint adventure contract. Then with FedEx. I tried to work with a

Vietnamese post office. A lot of them. I actually like my life in Vietnam now. It was okay for me to live in Vietnam for the rest of my life.

But there is one thing I changed my mind for: my daughter never could go to college. Because to get into a college, she needed to pass a college entrance exam for a limit of college seats. It did not measure the amount of knowledge the student had. It made the person believe that it was some way to qualify people for college.

Before 1989, the basis of acceptance to college was the history of the family. Not academic skills. She would not be allowed into college because of my military allegiance. I will tell you that at that time, the American Government tried to help the Communist's former Prisoners of War, to resettle in another country, especially the United States.

According to an agreement between the Communist Government and the United States Government, they selected a number of former prisoners. They were given priority to settle in the United States.

But I refused to go. First of all, I thought I did not speak English very well. I could not begin my life in a different country where I knew nothing about the culture, about the things I would need to do to survive. If I were to go to France, I would be able to

TRUC TRAN: My Story of a District Attorney in War

practice law. I studied the French Law System. My wife said no very quickly. She did not want to go. So, I told them, I'm sorry.

One day, my daughter came to me and said, "Daddy, let's go to the United States of America so that I can get an education."

Oh, I decided immediately, "Yes!" I submitted my application thirty days before my window of opportunity expired. I barely made it. After one year, we were on board to the United States. My wife was on the list to come here as a refugee. She decided not to go. She was afraid to die in the airplane.

I chose to come to Nashville, Tennessee just because my sister and her family had come here 3 years before. The first and most important reason for me choosing Nashville was because her children had a very successful education experience. For just 5 years (in 1998) coming to the United States as a refugee, her first daughter graduated from Tennessee State University, where she received a BS degree (summa cum laude) in Chemistry with a perfect 4.0 GPA. "The Middle" son graduated from Vanderbilt University with a double degree (cum laude) in Chemical Engineering & Applied Mathematics. And the youngest daughter was heading to pharmacy school at Mercer University in Atlanta, Georgia where she received (magna cum laude) her Doctor of Pharmacy in 2002.

So, I think that Nashville is a good place for everything. I decided to go to Nashville- Capital of The State of Tennessee.

Truc Tran & Winston Vo

My Nashville Home

First, I lived with her in a small house, our two families, my daughter and I and she and her family. I slept in the living room on the floor. My daughter and my nieces shared a bedroom. Early in the mornings, they would go to college, and everything was fine with us. Many people live in a small house.

When I came over here, I received food stamps. Friends of mine told me you can get food stamps to live for a little while until you adjust to the change. They told me to relax and enjoy some time off. But after one month, I felt that I needed a job.

The first job I got was at Christie Cookie Co. A place near the Tennessee State University campus. They make cakes. I boxed the cakes they made. After two or three weeks, I got a job with Jamison Bedding Company as a janitor. After I finished making coffee and everything, I would help the people in the factory to fold the materials or bag the mattresses. At the same time, I got a job as a janitor in the Centennial Medical Center at night. Every day, I would leave the house at 6:00 am in the morning and return at 9:00 pm at night. They paid me at Jamison $5.40 an hour. At Centennial, they paid me $5.00 an hour at night.

One day, they asked me and another janitor who worked in the building to do the work that four janitors had previously done.

TRUC TRAN: My Story of a District Attorney in War

We agreed to do this. But we did not have enough time to do all the work.

We could not satisfy everybody. So almost every day they complained to us. We could not finish what they wanted us to do. One day, I felt bad because, in my country, they used to evaluate people on two bases: how you perform your obligations and how you treat other people. I could not stand the complaining almost every day. I could not do better because we were only two people. We couldn't do everything in the amount of time we were given. I told them I quit. Before I quit, I wrote a note to one of the tenants. A physician's office.

The following week, when I came back to get my check, the lady in that office asked me why.

She said, "Please don't quit."

I don't know why the people in that office were so very nice to me. When they received my note, they called the people who were responsible for the hiring.

They asked them, "Why did they quit?"

They told the people that we wanted a job with good pay and that they could not afford to pay us more.

I received a note from the tenants in the physician's office. They were happy for me because I left to find a better job. When I came back to talk with them, she cried and cried. I have kept those letters. They say something precious to me.

When I came over here, I met a lot of people who tried to disrespect me, at the same time, I met a lot of people who cared for me and turned me into an optimistic person. I believed that this was a good place for me to live. Some days, I worked at night in the H.G. Hill Food Store, while I worked in the Jamison Bedding Company in the daytime.

One day, Dr. Bahr Weiss, a friend of mine, both he and his wife are professors at Vanderbilt University, called me and told me he had found a job for me. He was talking about the job in Metro's ESL Department. I remember. I will never forget the resume.

Ms. Sue Reynolds called me for an appointment. I did not know where the Board of Education was. Dr. Bahr came to get me and took me to the Board of Education. He stayed in his car during the summertime, waiting for me while I was being interviewed by Ms. Reynolds. After that, whenever I needed help, he and his wife would help me. Anything I needed. They are that nice. Now they are our family friends.

Now, I work for the ESL program. I came in 1998. I worked for Hillsboro High School, West End Middle School, and several elementary schools in Nashville. At that time, they did not offer benefits to translators. Now, I have health insurance. But I needed benefits for my daughter and myself.

One day, I talked with the Manager of H.G. Hills in Green Hills. I told him the truth. I told him I need benefits. I asked him to put me on full-time work. I knew that they did not need a bagger for full-time. I was a bagger at the store. They gave me a full-time job with benefits.

I think it is because I was a good employee. Even though I was new, the way I do for the customer, pleased them. A lot of customers like me. Finally, they knew that I used to be a lawyer. And sometimes, a customer who speaks French will speak with me in French. They knew that I was an educated man.

I was satisfied with what I had. I liked working in the schools. I tried to do a good job at H.G. Hills. This is the way I was raised. To do my best. Another thing, I need to do whatever I can to get the customer to come and shop at Hills. There is just one thing. I always feel that I have a debt of gratitude to the store to the Manager as I do everything. Whatever they want me to do.

I'm known to all the people in that area. I'm famous. Everybody who comes to the store knows my name. They say a lot of good things to me.

The customer asked me, "Why do you work so hard? You are the best employee in this store. You are the asset of this store. You are the jewel of this store."

He said that. That was very important to me. The customer is important. I explained to the customer that the first reason is my culture.

In my country, there is a saying that goes, "You need to protect the tree that gives you food."

I think H.G. Hills is my tree. The tree that gives me food. The manager is the tree that gives me food. So, I need to do everything to protect H.G. Hills.

There is another saying that says, "If you drink the water, you need to know the source of the water."

My daughter has obtained a good education. She has a job with good pay. H.G. Hills is the source. Now I have a nice house. Now I have everything because the people at H. G. Hills gave it to me. Many times, my daughter has told me not to work so hard because we don't need that much money anymore. But I told her, you need to know who helped us so that today we have everything. I need to work for them.

I also like to be busy. I don't want to just sit around the house all day. The important reason is that I like to work in that area. Most of the people know me and most of the people like me. They like me.

Many people tell me, "I come here because of you! Because you are always nice to me!"

I do whatever they need me to do.

So, I have been working two jobs, just like that. Maybe because I'm getting old, I don't listen to music anymore. I don't like to watch movies. I just like to watch the news. I want to meditate. I want to read philosophy.

I think that's enough story. But maybe there is more story to tell you.

One day, you know, when I was in (I don't remember the name. I'm getting old) the prison in the North.

The story about eating Sweet Potatoes. He ate too many. So many that he had to throw up, but he didn't because he would have been shot for eating food he shouldn't. He sat with his back to the guards and stuffed himself so full that it made him sick. He couldn't do anything about being sick.

PROLOG

Mr. Tran has honored the name his parents presented him with.

About The Author

Truc Tran: a District Attorney (before 1975) in Quy Nhon and Hue Provinces. See his full CV in an outline below. He is my uncle.

Winston Hieu-Duc Vo, a Chemical Engineer- schooled at Vanderbilt and Johns Hopkins. Born in 1972 at DaNang, Vietnam. Dad- So Huu Vo had just moved here for a new appointment as Principal of Truong Van Hoa Quan Doi (school for Militants' children).

Moved to Saigon in 8th Grade after Dad returned home from the Re-education Camp. Admitted to The Polytechnic University of Saigon in 1990 with majoring in Civil Engineering and was awarded a full scholarship of tuition and a stipend for earning high scores from a college entrance exam. Arrived in the United States in 1992 under an H.O. #13 Program for Dad. In 1998, graduated cum laude in a double degree of Chemical Engineering & Applied Mathematics from Vanderbilt University. Worked for Honeywell Inc in Texas.

****

Some sketched CV of my uncle- Truc Tran

A Candidate (1996) for Legal Counsel

for the US Embassy in Hanoi

Before 1975

Bachelor of Law (Cu Nhan Luat) in Hue University-School of Law, 1964

Prosecutor at Military Courts in Quang Tri & Hue Provinces

District Attorney (Bien Ly) in Quy Nhon and Hue Provinces

After released from the Re-education Camp in 1984 (9 years)

Legal Advisor for Joint Stock Electronics Tien-Dat Company

Staff Lawyer for Russin & Vecchi Law Firm

Instructor in Contract Law at Open University (a British model) in Saigon.

Permitted to immigrate to the United States in 1995 with his daughter (at first, for study purpose). His wife still stayed in Vietnam.

Arriving in the United States in 1995

A Candidate (1996) for Legal Counsel for the US Embassy in Hanoi with supports from Dr. Bahr Weiss, a Psychology Professor at Vanderbilt University; Mr. Bob Clement, a US Representative from Tennessee; and Vecchi- a partner of Russin & Vecchi Law Firm in Saigon.

Truc Tran & Winston Vo

****

Some sketched CV of my dad- So Huu Vo

Before 1975

(Born from a farmer's family in a village in Hue.)

Quoc Hoc, Hue (1957)

Bachelor of Law (Cu Nhan Luat) in Hue University- School of Law (1959-ranked 1st & 1968)

Principal of Bo-De (Buddhist) High School in Quang Tri Province (1959-1966) at the age of 24.

Elected as Head Representative (Khoa 22- Khoa Tong Dong Vien) Thu-Duc Military Academy (1966)

Chief- Judicial Military Police (MP) in Quang Tri - Hue - DaNang

Principal of Van Hoa Quan Doi in DaNang (school for Militants' children) (1971-1975); in -- /1975, approved for joining The Office of The Military Attache- (Major General) in Saigon but waived for my youngest sister soon to be born- April 7, 1975, in Vung Tau. Cindy Ngan-Ha Vo now, is a pharmacist in Montreal, Canada. (PharmD, Mercer University 2002)

After released from the Re-education Camp in 1982 (7 years)

TRUC TRAN: My Story of a District Attorney in War

A merchant for schooler and worker's backpacks

Joined in as a member (Social Studies) of an elite academic group, named Center for Research and Translation Services (Trung Tam Nghien Cuu va Dich Thuat), District 3, Saigon

Electronic Instructor at The Electronics Apprenticeship School at Dakao (District 1, Saigon)

(My dad's student was the owner, and gave him books for self-study)

Enrolled in "A Refreshment Course about Socialism for High-Ranking Cadres" at the above center (my dad's residency status (in Saigon) was still illegal) with a thesis: "Analyze The Tale of Kieu by Nguyen Du" under The Scope of Marxist-Leninist"

Dad was ranked 1st and was honored to deliver a speech at its commencement address.

Joined in a new business of Newspapers and Books Wholesaler, and leased a Book Boutique next to Gia Long High School

Refused to be a partner with a graduate from School of Business Administration (Quoc Gia Hanh Chanh) to open a legal service. My dad has a law degree but has not practiced yet under the South Vietnam Government.

Immigrated to the United States in 1992 under the H.O. #13 program.

Made in the USA
Columbia, SC
28 February 2024